Edition Schott

Louis R. Feuillard

1872 – 1941

Daily Exercises
Tägliche Übungen
Exercices journaliers

for Violoncello
für Violoncello
pour violoncello

ED 1117
ISMN 979-0-001-03260-5

www.schott-music.com

Mainz · London · Madrid · Paris · New York · Tokyo · Beijing

Übungen für die linke Hand und den Bogen.
Triller, Tonleitern, Akkorde, Doppelgriffe usw.

1. Teil Übungen in den Halslagen
2. Teil Übungen, die das Violoncello in seiner ganzen Ausdehnung umfassen
3. Teil Übungen mit Daumenaufsatz
4. Teil Doppelgriffe
5. Teil Bogenübungen

Man spiele täglich einige Übungen aus jedem der fünf Teile; jede Übung zuerst langsam und beschleunige dann das Tempo immer mehr, achte dabei jedoch sehr auf die Gleichmäßigkeit.

*

Exercices pour la main gauche et l'archet.
Trilles, gammes, arpèges, doubles cordes etc.

1ère Partie Exercices aux positions du manche
2e Partie Exercices dans toute l'étendue du Violoncelle
3e Partie Exercices aux positions du pouce
4e Partie Doubles cordes
5e Partie Exercices d'archet

Travailler chaque jour quelques exercices dans chacune des cinq parties; chaque exercice d'abord lentement puis de plus en plus vite mais toujours très également.

*

Exercises for the left hand and bow.
Trills, Scales, Arpeggios, Double stopping etc.

1st Part Exercises in the neck positions
2nd Part Exercises in the whole compass of the cello
3rd Part Exercises in the thumb positions
4th Part Double stopping
5th Part Bowing Exercises

Examples from each of the five parts should be studied daily. The exercises should be practised slowly at first gradually increasing the speed. Care should be taken that they are played very evenly.

1. Teil
Übungen in den Halslagen

1ère Partie
Exercices aux positions du manche

1st Part
Exercises in the neck positions

1

Trillerübungen | **Exercices de Trilles** | Exercises in shakes

Varianten *Variantes* Variations

etc. etc. etc. etc.

Diese Studien sollen auf jeder Saite und in allen Lagen geübt werden.

Travailler ces exercices sur chaque corde et à toutes les positions.

These exercises should be studied on each string, and in all the positions.

Beispiel *Exemple* Example IIa IIIa IVa

2. Lage *2e position* 2nd position

3. Lage *3e position* 3rd position

4. Lage *4e position* 4th position

2

Ausführung
Exécution
Execution
1 Lage *1ère position* 1st position
Auf allen Saiten zu üben.
Travailler ces exercices sur chaque corde.
These exercises should be studied on all the strings.
Beispiel
Exemple
Example
IIa
IIIa
IVa
etc.

3

1. u. 2. Lage *1ère et 2e positions* 1st & 2nd positions

4

1. u. 3. Lage *1ère et 3e positions* 1st & 3rd positions

2. u. 3. Lage 2e. et 3e. positions 2nd & 3rd positions
5
1. u. 4. Lage 1ère et 4e. positions 1st & 4th positions

2. u. 4. Lage *2e et 4e positions* 2nd & 4th positions
21
22
23
24
25
26
27
28
29
30
31
32
33
34
35
36
37
38
39
40
3. u. 4. Lage *3e et 4e positions* 3rd & 4th positions
41
42
43
44
45
simile
46
47
48
49
50
51
52
53
54
55
56
57
58
59
60
61
62
63

6

1. u. 5. Lage *1ère et 5e positions* 1st & 5th positions
III a.
IV a.
II a.
2. u. 5. Lage *2e et 5e positions* 2nd & 5th positions
3. u. 5. Lage *3e et 5e positions* 3rd & 5th positions
4. u. 5. Lage *4e et 5e positions* 4th & 5th positions
simile

7

1. u. 6. Lage *1ère et 6e positions* 1st & 6th positions
simile
IIa
IIIa
IVa
2. u. 6. Lage *2e et 6e positions* 2nd & 6th positions
3. u. 6. Lage *3e et 6e positions* 3rd & 6th positions
4. u. 6. Lage *4e et 6e positions* 4th & 6th positions
simile
5. u. 6. Lage *5e et 6e positions* 5th & 6th positions

8

Übungen in allen Halslagen

Exercices à toutes les positions du manche

Exercises in all the neck positions

Man spiele diese Übungen in allen Tonarten
Travailler ces exercises dans tous les tons
These exercises should be studied in all the keys

9

Varianten *Variantes* Variations
Man spiele diese Übungen in allen Tonarten
Travailler ces exercices dans tous les tons
These exercises should be studied in all the keys
etc.

10

Tonleitern durch 2 Oktaven | **Gammes à deux octaves** | Scales of 2 octaves

Fis
Fa♯
F♯
G
Sol
G
As
La♭
A♭
A
La♮
A
B
Si♭
B♭
H
Si♮
B

11

Akkorde durch 2 Oktaven | **Arpèges à deux octaves** | Arpeggios of 2 octaves

C
Do ♮
C

Cis
Do ♯
C♯

D
Ré
D

Es
Mi ♭
E♭

E
Mi ♮
E

F
Fa ♮
F

Fis
Fa ♯
F♯
IIa
G
Sol
G
As
La ♭
A♭
A
La ♮
A
B
Si ♭
B♭
H
Si ♮
B

12

Terzen | Tierces | Thirds

13

Übungen in allen Tonarten

Ausführung: Man übe zuerst jeden Takt mehrmals einzeln; hierauf spiele man die 8 Takte aufeinanderfolgend, so daß sie eine für sich abgeschlossene Übung bilden.

Exercices dans tous les tons

Execution: Travailler plusieurs fois chaque mesure, ensuite enchainer les 8 mesures sans arrêt.

Exercises in all keys

Method: Play each bar several times, then join the 8 bars together.

Fis
Fa ♯
F♯
II○
G
Sol
G
As
La♭
A♭
A
La♮
A
B
Si♭
B♭
H
Si♮
B

14

Chromatische Übungen | **Exercices chromatiques** | Chromatic exercises

15

Übungen um die Geläufigkeit der Finger zu entwickeln

Man spiele mehrere Wiederholungen auf einen Bogen.

Exercices pour développer l'agilité des doigts

Faire plusieurs fois chaque reprise dans un même coup d'archet.

Exercises to develope the agility of the fingers

Repeat each bar several times in one bow.

2. Teil

Übungen, die das Violoncell in seiner ganzen Ausdehnung umfassen

2e. Partie

Exercices dans toute l'étendue du Violoncelle

2nd. Part

Exercises in the whole compass of the Cello

16

Varianten *Variantes* Variations

Man spiele diese Übungen in allen Tonarten
Travailler ces exercices dans tous les tons
These exercises should be studied in all the keys

etc.

17

Tonleitern durch zwei Oktaven, auf einer Saite, mit zwei, bei allen Tonleitern anwendbaren Fingersätzen

Gammes a deux octaves sur une seule corde avec deux doigtés applicables a toutes les gammes

Scales of two octaves on one string with an alternative fingering

E
Mi ♮
E
F
Fa ♮
F
Fis
Fa ♯
Fa ♯
G
Sol
G
As
La ♭
A ♭
A
La ♮
A
Chromatic Chromatique Chromatic

18

Akkorde durch zwei Octaven auf einer Saite	**Arpèges à deux octaves sur une seule corde**	Arpeggios of two octaves on one string

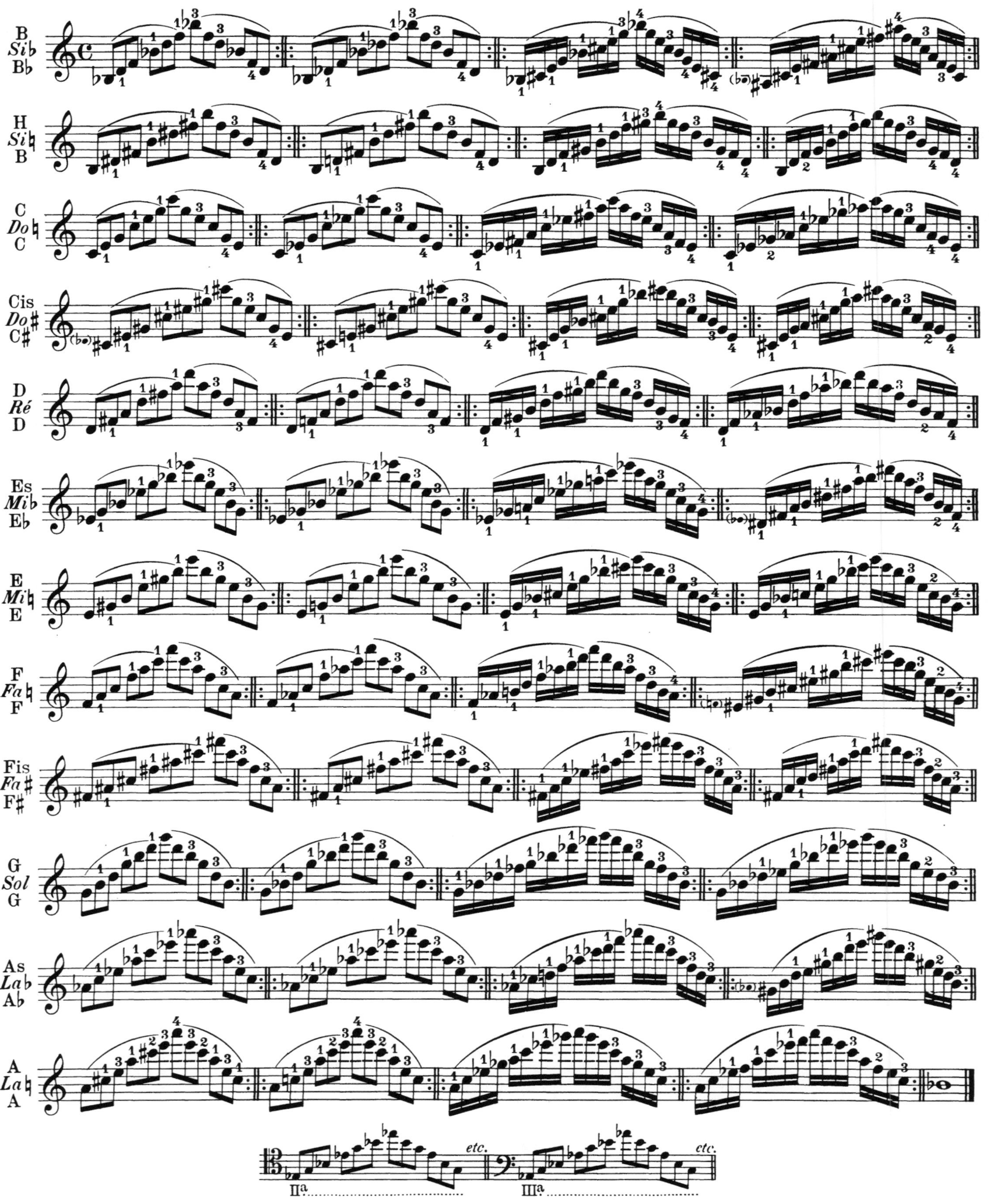

19

Tonleitern

Die Tonleitern sind mit zweierlei Fingersätzen bezeichnet und zwar
1.) mit dem meistenteils angewendeten (siehe Nº 20)
2.) mit einem neuen Fingersatz, (siehe Nº 19) der durch seine Einfachheit die Ausführung der Tonleitern erleichtern wird.

Es genügt, wenn man sich den Platz des 1. Fingers am Anfang der Tonleiter merkt und dann, nach jeweils drei Noten, die Lage der Hand verändert.
1.) Bei den Tonleitern durch 2 Oktaven greift man die 1. Note immer mit dem 1. Finger.
2.) Bei den Tonleitern durch 3 Oktaven greift man die 2. Note immer mit dem 1. Finger.
3.) Bei den Tonleitern durch 4 Oktaven greift man die 3. Note immer mit dem 1. Finger.

Gammes

Les gammes sont données avec deux doigtés:
1º Celui du Nº 20 qui est le plus généralement employé
2º Celui du Nº 19 est un nouveau doigté qui par sa simplicité facilitera l'éxécution des gammes.

Il suffira de se rappeler la place du 1er doigt au début de la gamme et ensuite de déplacer la main toutes les trois notes.
1º Pour les gammes à 2 octaves le premier doigt est toujours sur la 1ère note.
2º Pour les gammes à 3 octaves le premier doigt est toujours sur la 2e note.
3º Pour les gammes à 4 octaves le premier doigt est toujours sur la 3e note.

Scales

The scales are given with two fingerings.
1. That of Nº 20 (most generally used)
2. Nº 19, a new fingering, which by its simplicity facilitates the execution of the scales.

It is sufficient to remember the position of the 1st finger at the beginning of the scale, then change position every three notes.
1) For scales of 2 octaves the 1st finger is always on the 1st note.
2) For scales of 3 octaves the 1st finger is always on the 2nd note.
3) For scales of 4 octaves the 1st finger is always on the 3rd note.

Tonleitern durch zwei Oktaven mit demselben Fingersatz bei allen Tonleitern

Gammes à deux octaves avec le même doigté pour toutes les gammes

Scales of two octaves with the same fingering for all keys

Über die Tonleitern durch 2 Oktaven auf einer Saite siehe Nº 15.

Pour les gammes à deux octaves sur la même corde Voir Nº 15.

For scales of 2 octaves on one string, see Nº 15.

Tonleitern durch drei Oktaven mit demselben Fingersatz bei allen Tonleitern

Gammes à trois octaves avec le même doigté pour toutes les gammes

Scales of three octaves with the same fingering for all keys

Tonleitern durch vier Oktaven mit demselben Fingersatz bei allen Tonleitern

Gammes à quatre octaves avec le même doigté pour toutes les gammes

Scales of four octaves with the same fingering for all keys

Moll Tonleitern | Gammes mineures | Minor Scales

20

Tonleitern durch 3 u. 4 Oktaven	**Gammes à 3 et 4 octaves**	Scales of 3 & 4 octaves
1.) Bei den Tonleitern durch 4 Oktaven kann man die beiden angegebenen Fingersätze verwenden.	*1º Pour les gammes à 4 octaves on peut employer les deux doigtés indiqués.*	1) For scales of 4 octaves both the fingerings indicated can be used.
2.) Bei den Tonleitern durch 3 Oktaven wende man die Fingersätze unter den Noten an.	*2º Pour les gammes à 3 octaves n'employer que le doigté placé au dessous des notes.*	2) For scales of 3 octaves use the fingering printed below the notes.

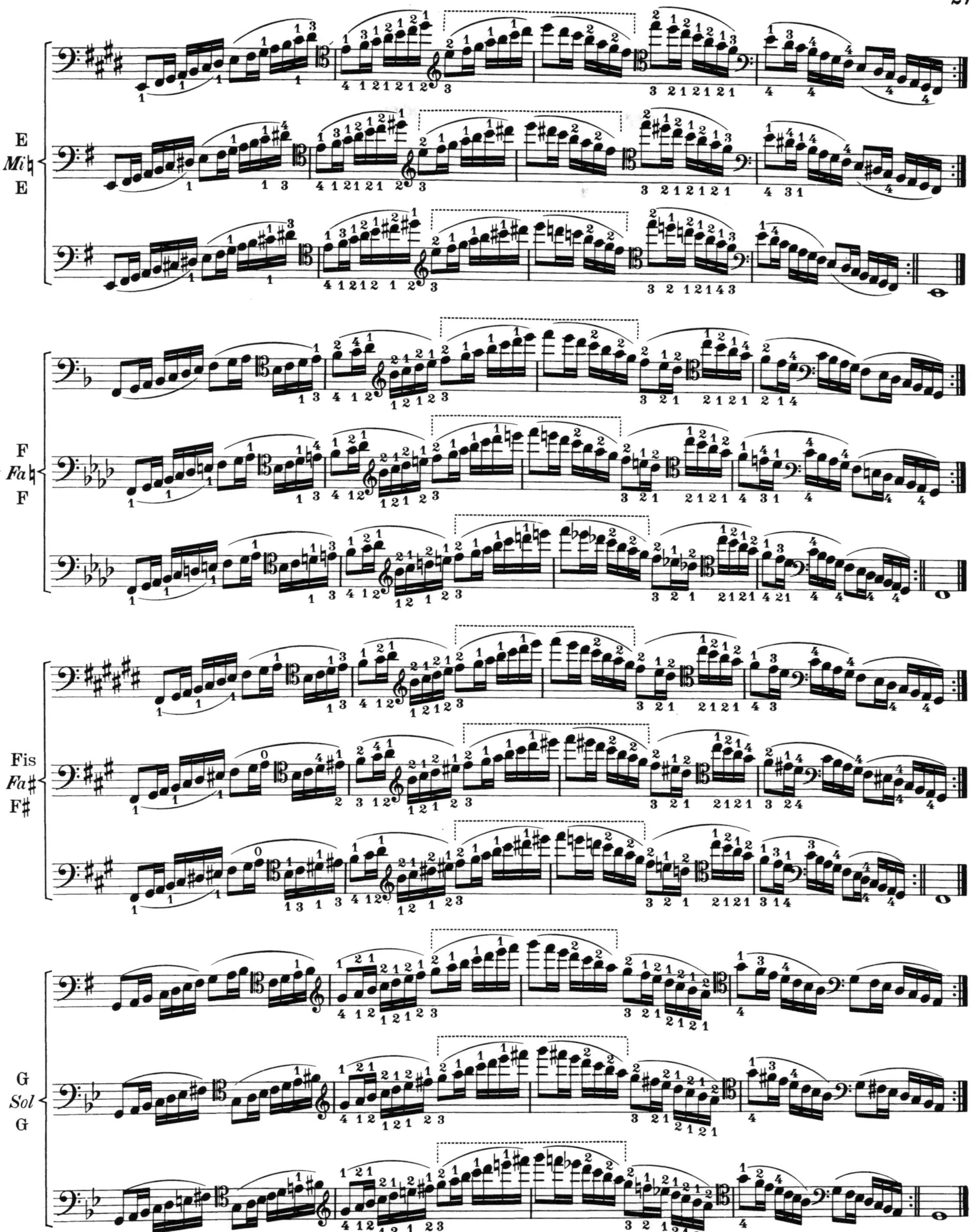
E
Mi♮
E
F
Fa♮
F
Fis
Fa♯
F♯
G
Sol
G

As
La♭
A♭
A
La♮
A
B
Si♭
B♭
H
Si♮
B

21

Akkorde durch vier Oktaven | Arpèges à quatre octaves | Arpeggios of four octaves

E
Mi ♮
E
F
Fa ♮
F
Fis
Fa ♯
F♯
G
Sol
G

As
La♭
A♭
A
La♮
A
B
Si♭
B♭
H
Si♮
B

22

Akkord=Übungen | Exercices en arpèges | Arpeggio Exercises

23

Tonleitern und Akkorde
wie man sie häufig in der modernen Musik antrifft.

Gammes et Arpèges
que l'on rencontre fréquemment dans la musique moderne.

Scales & Arpeggios
frequently met with in modern music.

Die Tonleitern auf: D, E, Fis, As, B sind identisch mit der Tonleiter auf C.
Die Tonleitern auf: Es, F, G, A, H sind identisch mit der Tonleiter auf Cis.

Les gammes de Re, Mi♮, Fa♯, Lab, Sib. sont identiques à la gamme de Do♮.
Les gammes de Mi♭, Fa♮, Sol, La♮, Si♮ sont identiques à la gamme de Do♯.

The scales of D, E, F♯, A♭, B♭ are identical with the scale of C.
The scales of E♭, F, G, A, B are identical with the scale of C♯.

3. Teil
Übungen mit Daumenaufsatz

3e Partie
Exercices aux positions du pouce

3rd Part
Exercises in the thumb positions

24

Man spiele diese Übungen in allen Tonarten
Travailler ces exercices dans tous les tons
These exercises should be studied in all the keys

26

Tonleitern | Gammes | Scales

A *La* ♮ A

B *Si* ♭ B♭

H *Si* ♮ B

C *Do* ♮ C

Cis *Do* ♯ C♯

D *Ré* D

Es *Mi* ♭ E♭

E *Mi* ♮ E

F *Fa* F

Fis *Fa* ♯ F♯

G *Sol* G

As *La* ♭ A♭

27

Akkorde | **Arpèges** | Arpeggios

IIª Iª

A
La ♮
A

B
Si ♭
B♭

H
Si ♮
B

C
Do ♮
C

Cis
Do ♯
C♯

D
Ré
D

Es
Mi ♭
E♭

E
Mi ♮
E

F
Fa ♮
F

Fis
Fa ♯
F♯

G
Sol
G

As
La ♭
A♭

4. Teil

Doppelgriffe

4e Partie

Doubles cordes

4th Part

Double stopping

28

Übungen um die Finger unabhängig zu machen, und zur Vorbereitung der Doppelgriffe

Die ganzen Noten sollen wohl gegriffen, aber nicht angestrichen werden.

Exercices pour acquérir l'indépendance des doigts et préparer aux doubles cordes

Il faut tenir les rondes sans les jouer.

Exercises to acquire independence of the fingers & to prepare for double stopping

The semibreves to be stopped with the fingers, but not played with the bow.

Ausführung
Exécution
Execution

A

B

29

Doppelgriffe | **Doubles cordes** | **Double stopping**

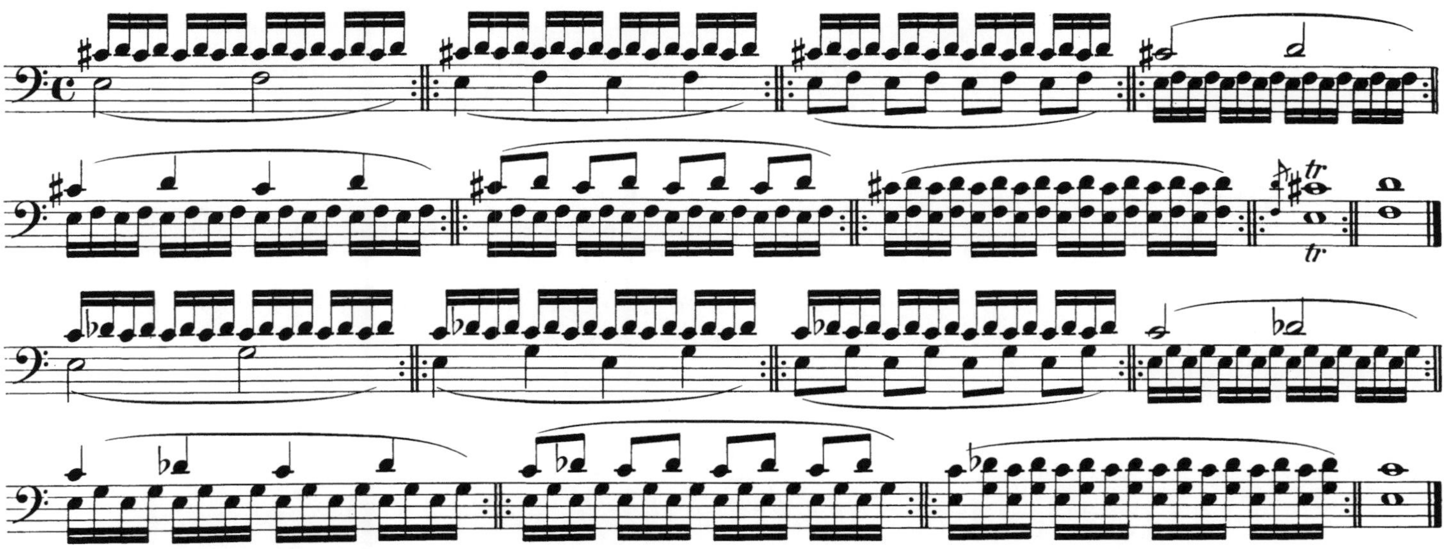

Doppelgriffe mit ungleichen Notenwerten

Man spiele die Übungen 1 u. 2 sehr langsam, und zähle dazu; dann beschleunige man das Zeitmaß bis man zu 1bis und 2bis gelangt.

Valeurs inégales en doubles cordes

Travailler les exercices 1 et 2 très lentement en comptant les temps puis accélérer le mouvement pour arriver aux 1bis et 2bis

Unequal values in double stopping

Study the exercises 1 & 2 very slowly at first, gradually increasing the speed until arriving at 1bis & 2bis

30

Terzen, Sexten und Oktaven | **Tierces, sixtes et octaves** | Thirds, sixths & octaves

1 Oktave *1 octave* 1 octave

Sexten *Sixtes* Sixthes

etc.

2 Oktaven *2 octaves* 2 octaves

etc.

3 Oktaven *3 octaves* 3 octaves

Tonleitern *Gammes* Scales

Oktaven *Octaves* Octaves

IIa

etc.

Terzen *Tierces* Thirds

etc.

Akkorde *Arpèges* Arppeggios

Terzen *Tierces* Thirds

etc.

Ia IIa

etc.

31

Natürliche und künstliche Flageolettöne | **Sons harmoniques naturels et artificiels** | Natural & Artifical harmonics

A Ia IIa etc. IIIa etc. IVa etc.

B Ia

etc. Und so fort in allen Tonarten
Continuer dans tous les tons
Continue in other keys

5. Teil

Bogenübungen

Abkürzungen:

- ⊓ Herunterstrich
- V Hinaufstrich
- G Ganzer Bogen
- M In der Mitte
- Fr Am Frosch
- Sp An der Spitze
- H Halber Bogen

5e Partie

Exercices d'archet

Abréviations:

- ⊓ *Tirez*
- V *Poussez*
- G *Tout l'archet*
- M *Au milieu*
- Fr *Au talon*
- Sp *A la pointe*
- H *La moitié de l'archet*

5th Part

Bowing Exercises

Abbreviations:

- ⊓ Down bow
- V Up bow
- G Whole length of bow
- M In Middle
- Fr At the nut
- Sp At the point
- H Half length of bow

32

Übungen für den rechten Arm

Exercices pour le bras droit

Exercises for the right arm

33

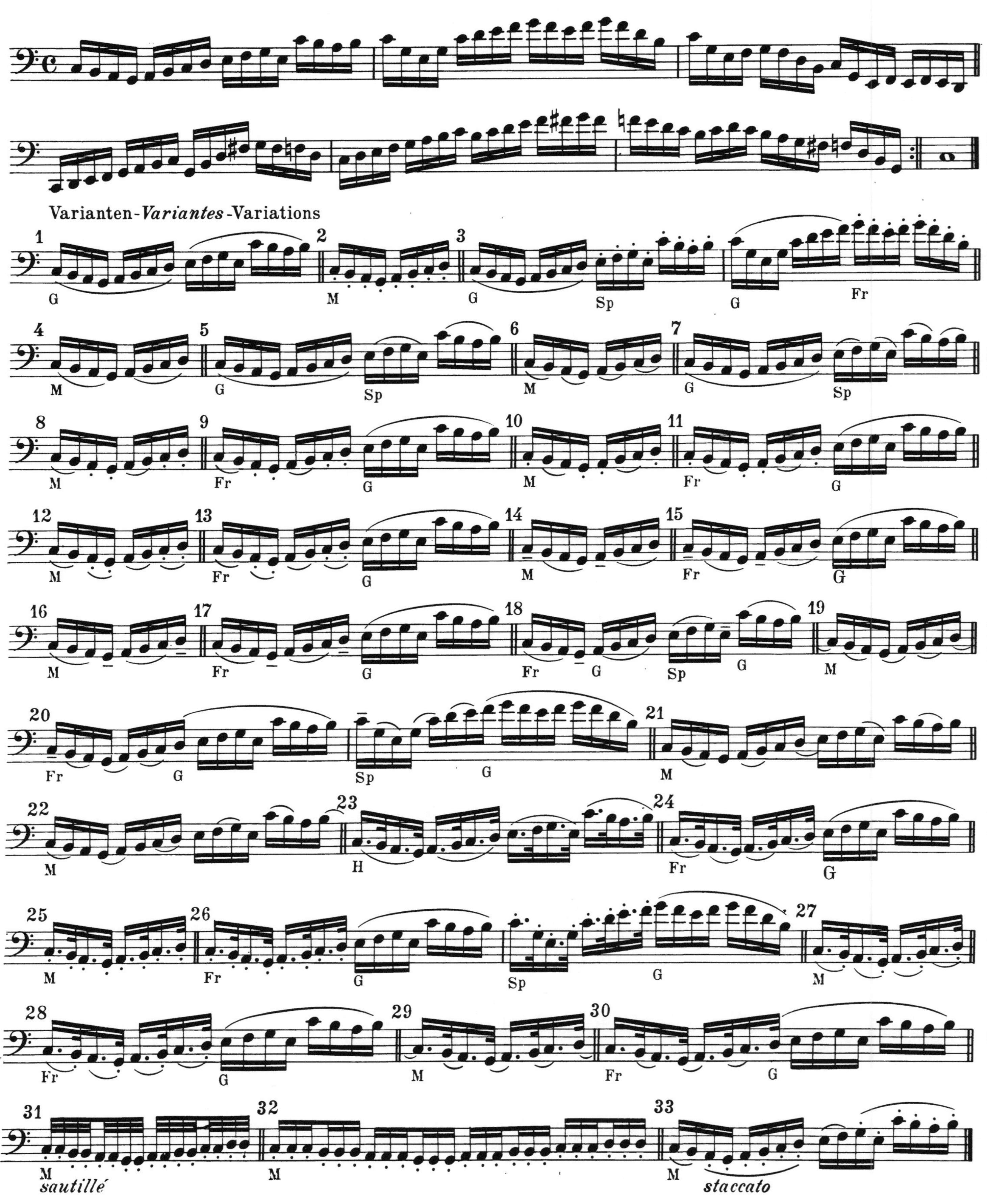
Varianten-Variantes-Variations
sautillé
staccato

34

Übungen um die Geschmeidigkeit des Handgelenks zu entwickeln

Exercices pour développer la souplesse du poignet

Exercises for developing suppleness of wrist

35

Übungen auf drei Saiten | **Exercices sur trois cordes** | Exercises on three strings

36

Übungen um die Kraft des Handgelenks zu entwickeln

Exercices pour développer la force du poignet

Exercises for developing the power of the wrist

Variante *Variantes* Variations

1 *f* G 2 *etc.* 3 4

5 *f* G 6 7 8 9

10 11 H G H G 12 M 13 Fr G Sp G 14 M

15 M 16 17 18 19 20

21 M 22 G 23 M 24 G 25 H

26 G 27 28 M 29 M

30 M 31 32 33 Fr G Sp G

34 G 35 36 37

38 M 39 G 40 Fr 41 G 42 *Sautillé* M